MW00891084

Happy Holidays!

Holi

by Betsy Rathburn

BELLWETHER MEDIA
MINNEAPOLIS, MN

Blastoff! Beginners are developed by literacy experts and educators to meet the needs of early readers. These engaging informational texts support young children as they begin reading about their world. Through simple language and high frequency words paired with crisp, colorful photos, Blastoff! Beginners launch young readers into the universe of independent reading.

Blastoff! Universe

Reading Level — Grade K — Blastoff! Beginners

Grades 1-3 — Blastoff! Readers

Grade 4 — Blastoff! Discovery

Sight Words in This Book 🔍

a	is	people	to
and	it	see	water
eat	of	the	with
go	on	they	
in	out	time	

This edition first published in 2024 by Bellwether Media, Inc.

No part of this publication may be reproduced in whole or in part without written permission of the publisher. For information regarding permission, write to Bellwether Media, Inc., Attention: Permissions Department, 6012 Blue Circle Drive, Minnetonka, MN 55343.

Library of Congress Cataloging-in-Publication Data

LC record for Holi available at: https://lccn.loc.gov/2023001663

Text copyright © 2024 by Bellwether Media, Inc. BLASTOFF! BEGINNERS and associated logos are trademarks and/or registered trademarks of Bellwether Media, Inc.

Editor: Christina Leaf   Designer: Laura Sowers

Printed in the United States of America, North Mankato, MN.

Table of Contents

It Is Holi!

Bright colors
fill the air.
It is Holi!

4

Welcome Spring!

Holi is in February or March. It welcomes spring.

It is on a
full moon.
Hindus
honor Holi.

Full of Color

People light
bonfires.
They sing
and dance.

bonfire

People go out
to the street.
They spray water.

They throw
colored **powder**!

powder

People spend time with family.
They see friends.

17

People eat
fried **dumplings**.
They eat
sweet pancakes.

pancakes

dumplings

Holi is a
fun holiday.
It is full of color!

Holi Facts

Celebrating Holi

family

powder

dumplings

Holi Activities

light
bonfires

throw
colored
powder

eat fried
dumplings

Glossary

bonfires

big fires

dumplings

pockets of dough stuffed with meat, fruits, or vegetables

Hindus

people who practice Hinduism

powder

a fine dust

To Learn More

ON THE WEB

FACTSURFER

Factsurfer.com gives you a safe, fun way to find more information.

1. Go to www.factsurfer.com.

2. Enter "Holi" into the search box and click 🔍.

3. Select your book cover to see a list of related content.

Index

The images in this book are reproduced through the courtesy of: Greg Brave, front cover; StockImageFactory, p. 3; Kristin F. Ruhs, pp. 4-5; StanislavBeloglazov, pp. 6-7; Abhishek Sah Photography, pp. 8-9; Sumit Saraswat, pp. 10-11; MindStorm, pp. 12-13; Vandathai, p. 14; Ruzely Abdullah, pp. 14-15; Prasannapix, p. 16; Stock Exchange, pp. 16-17; Indian Creations, p. 18; Rangeech, pp. 18-19; SoumenNath, pp. 20-21; PhotosIndia.com LLC/ Alamy, p. 22 (celebrating, eat fried dumplings); Dipak Shelare, pp. 22 (light bonfires), 23 (bonfires); Mikhail Klyoshev, p. 22 (throw colored powder); Fotonium, p. 23 (dumplings); CreativeMinds2, p. 23 (Hindus); djero.adlibeshe yahoo.com, p. 23 (powder).